DITCH THE PITCH

AF473292

DITCH THE PITCH

STOP SELLING. START SERVING. *Grow* REFERRALS.

L. PAUL DORSEY

In memory of my brother-in-law, Bill Brennan,
who never pitched but always served—
in, on, and off the court.

DITCH THE PITCH

Stop Selling. Start Serving. Grow Referrals.

© 2026 by L. Paul Dorsey
All rights reserved.

Printed in the United States of America.

No part of this publication may be reproduced or distributed in any form or by any means without the prior permission of the publisher. Requests for permission should be directed to permissions@indiebooksintl.com or mailed to Permissions, Indie Books International, 2511 Woodlands Way, Oceanside, CA 92054.

The views and opinions in this book are those of the author at the time of writing this book, and do not reflect the opinions of Indie Books International or its editors.

Neither the publisher nor the author is engaged in rendering legal or other professional services through this book. If expert assistance is required, the services of appropriate professionals should be sought. The publisher and the author shall have neither liability nor responsibility to any person or entity with respect to any loss or damage caused directly or indirectly by the information in this publication.

Dunkin' Donuts® is a registered trademark of DD IP Holder, LLC.
Girl Scout Cookie® is a registered trademark of Girl Scouts of the United States of America.
Home Depot® is a registered trademark of Home Depot Product Authority, LLC.
Instagram® is a registered trademark of Instagram, LLC.
J.P. Morgan® is a registered trademark of JPMorgan Chase Bank, N.A.
Miller High Life® and Miller Lite® are registered trademarks of Molson Coors Beverage Company USA, LLC.
Peanuts® and Charlie Brown® are registered trademarks of Peanuts Worldwide, LLC.
Realtor® is a registered trademark of National Association of Realtors.
Reels® is a registered trademark of Meta Platforms, Inc.
Smith Barney® is a registered trademark of Morgan Stanley Domestic Holdings, LLC.
Taco Bell® is a registered trademark of Taco Bell IP Holder, LLC.
Target® is a registered trademark of Target Brands, Inc.
Tilt-a-Whirl® is a registered trademark of J&S Rides, Land & Equipment, LLC.

ISBN-13: 978-1-966168-76-8

Library of Congress Control Number: 2026907291

Cover design by Katie Dorsey
Interior designed by Melissa Farr, Back Porch Creative, LLC

INDIE BOOKS INTERNATIONAL®, INC.
2511 WOODLANDS WAY
OCEANSIDE, CA 92054
www.indiebooksintl.com

Table Of Contents

PREFACE

Why "Stop Selling" Matters

As I write this, I watch an ant carry a muffin crumb, five times its size, across my windowsill. The sheer size of his bounty thwarts his ability to squeeze through the crack where the molding meets the window. He must be an amateur. It reminds me of myself at my first attempt as a financial advisor.

I thought it would be easy, having spent a tour in the Navy as a disbursing officer (think paymaster if you are an Army type). For you civilians out there, I paid the crew. My training consisted of customer service, customer service, and more customer service.

Entering the job market as a former naval officer responsible for millions of dollars, I thought the J.P. Morgans and Smith Barneys of the world would be all over me. *Not*. A relatively unknown, and now defunct, life insurance company would become the best hope for this 2.3 GPA math major with no industry experience.

I try to help the ant with the tip of my pen, but it's not the right tool. The ant abandons the muffin crumb and retreats into the crack.

The life insurance company tried to help me. Selling became the word of the day, every day. My on-the-job training consisted of sales pitches to unsuspecting friends or family. This was followed by cold calls to "orphan" clients whose previous advisors had abandoned them, failed out of the business, or starved to death due to lack of customers.

Three senior advisors carried the load of the entire office. They only talked about prospecting, selling, and closing. Nobody mentioned customer service. The rest of the amateur salespeople came and went, usually within a few months.

With no gray hair and less experience, I failed as miserably as this ant on my windowsill. Luckily, I failed forward, when a desperate trust company hired me as an entry-level securities processor. A friend said they must be running a sinking ship.

The company may have been taking on water, but it offered me experience in the advisor industry. Over the next ten years, our team turned the ship around. In the process, I survived the underbelly of investment operations, learning all aspects of stock dividends, sales, and fees.

We worked with financial advisors from all over the country, some good, others bad, and many self-serving. Plenty of them knew more about selling than they knew about investments. I still wanted to become one of them, but the lift seemed too big to start from zero.

The ant appears again on the windowsill to pick up the muffin crumb. It makes it to the crack and, like before, it gets stuck. This time, instead of poking it with my ballpoint pen, I lift it up with a piece of loose-leaf paper. He scrambles around my notes as I carry him outside and set him, complete with a crumb, on the sidewalk.

After a few years at the trust company, I met a senior advisor near the end of her career. She worked strictly on referrals, building long-term relationships by exceeding her customers' expectations. During a series of account reviews at her office, I witnessed the same hands-on customer service that I learned in the Navy. Her authenticity inspired me to make another run at a career as an advisor.

Maybe, if I took care of the first customer, that person would refer another, and one day the money would follow.

Twenty-five years later, our first client is still a customer. We can trace over 350 relationships back to her. They've all come by word of mouth, all referrals.

Along the way, we developed a service-oriented process built on exceeding expectations for each and every customer. We don't sell, nor do we ask for referrals.

Many successful financial advisors, Realtors, and lawyers use the same process. There is nothing new here. But when you're young, or starting a new career, or struggling for new accounts, nobody tells you how to be successful.

Using real-life stories and customer anecdotes, this book provides a map to success that I wish I had when I took my first job. As a friend's dad once so eloquently said, "Nothing's easy!"

Service trumps selling. Always. Hopefully, the anecdotes and processes in this book will accelerate your success.

The ant never returned. I like to think he became the largest crumb producer in his colony with a little help from my notes.

L. Paul Dorsey

CHAPTER 1

Hurricanes

An acoustic guitar player sings classic rock songs to mostly empty tables at the oldest pub in Delaware. From the far side of the room, my roommate Pete and I watch two young women strut in and perch themselves at the end of the bar.

Pete downs the last of his Miller Lite and says, "Let's go talk to those ladies."

"Not a good idea," I argue. "They're way out of our league."

"Everybody's out of your league." He slides his empty glass across the table and is on his way. "They like the same music."

Not wanting to be left at the table alone, I follow, shoulders slumped and hands in pockets.

Pete goes through the usual pleasantries. "Great guitar player. You guys from around here? Do you know so-and-so?"

Then I muster up the nerve to ask what kind of work they do. The tall one with hoop earrings gets serious. "We're 'hurricaneologists.'"

"Hurricaneologists? What the hell is that?"

"We name hurricanes."

The shorter girl with holes in her jeans lists a few. "This year we have Allison, Barry, Chantel, with a *C*, and Dean."

"*E*'s a hard one to pick. Erin or Elaine," says Hoop Earrings. "We went with Elaine."

Pete waves the bartender over. "Can we get a couple of hurricanes for our friends here?"

The conversation goes well, that is, until the ladies finish their cocktails.

"We have to get to work early tomorrow in case hurricane season runs long," says Holes In Her Jeans as she drops a dollar in the guitar player's tip jar.

"We're leaning toward Wanda for the *W* hurricane, but *X*, *Y*, and *Z* will be a challenge," says Hoop Earrings. Then they disappear.

I glare at Pete. "That was a bad investment of time and money."

He smiles. "We'll find out soon enough."

I squint back at him, not knowing I'm about to learn a simple lesson that will change my life for the better.

"I slipped her my number on the back of my business card. If she wants to hang out, she can call. It's all up to her."

"What?"

"One, it takes the pressure off me. And two, she's not used to being treated with that kind of respect."

"Wow."

"It's easier to let people choose you than for you to chase them."

So simple. Yet genius.

It's easier to let people choose you than for you to chase them.

Wouldn't it be great to have new customers chasing after you?

How much more time would you have to service existing customers if you didn't have to waste time looking for new ones?

CHAPTER 2

Customers

Enough about dating. Let's talk about business.

Why are big businesses, small businesses, and individual proprietors in business? To make money, of course.

How do businesses make money? They sell a product or service.

And who buys the product or service? The customer, of course.

Businesses sell products or services to customers to make money.

Businesses invest big money to improve their sales. Teaching how to sell is big business in itself.

Sales training runs in the top five categories of all corporate training investment. In the United States, businesses will spend approximately $3.44 billion on sales training in 2025. It's more than double that worldwide.[1]

Go to any sales meeting, whether it be attorneys, accountants, investment advisors, furniture salespeople or plumbers, you're going to hear about the prospect, the sale, and the close.

Pick up any book on sales. On the first few pages, you're going to read about the prospect, the sale, and the close.

Let's look at those three words from a customer perspective.

Think back to the first time you walked into a car dealership where you knew nobody on the inside.

As soon as you park your car in the designated spot, you see three salespeople standing around a cubicle. Each is checking you out through the oversized wall of glass. Wearing their camouflage quarter zips, they think you don't see them.

When you step through the big glass door, you feel like a deer lost from the herd, tiptoeing into an open field on the first day of hunting season. All three salespeople want the shot. They want to make the kill. They want to close the sale.

---

1 Coherent Market Insights Pvt. Ltd. "Sales Training Market Is Projected to Reach USD 16.91 Billion by 2032 | Coherent Market Insights." *GlobeNewswire News Room*, September 4, 2025. https://www.globenewswire.com/news-release/2025/09/04/3144701/0/en/Sales-Training-Market-is-Projected-to-Reach-USD-16-91-Billion-by-2032-Coherent-Market-Insights.html.

If you've ever had this experience, you know how it feels.

Would you let your grandmother go into a car dealer alone? *No.*

In October 2025, a CarEdge study found that 82 percent of respondents indicated low trust in dealerships.[2] Do you know how many people own a car in 2025? Almost everybody.

Americans are expected to purchase around 16 million cars in 2025.[3] And dealers will somehow frustrate upwards of 13 million people.

Here's what it means. Everybody wants to buy. Nobody likes to be sold. Yet when businesses discuss sales, they talk about a prospect. They forget about the humanness of the customer.

Everybody wants to buy. That's the opportunity.

Businesses focus on their business. Businesses forget they are in business for the customer. Companies use terms like "prospect," "sale," or "close," collectively referred to as the "PSC." These terms are jargon, selling jargon.

---

2 CarEdge. "CarEdge Car Buying Index: 82% of Americans Don't Trust Dealers - CarEdge," October 24, 2025. https://caredge.com/car-buying-index-october-2025.

3 S&P Global. "October 2025 US auto sales expected to moderate from elevated Q3 levels," October 29, 2025. Accessed November 7, 2025. https://www.spglobal.com/automotive-insights/en/blogs/2025/07/us-auto-sales.

And nobody likes to be sold.

James Carville, the lead strategist for Bill Clinton, helped Clinton win the presidency over George Bush with a simple saying.

"It's the economy, stupid!"

We still hear the same saying in every election cycle.

If James Carville specialized in business, he might say, "It's the customer, stupid!"

Customers aren't stupid. They're smart enough to see through the salespeople who act stupid. They sense when the rifle scope is on them, when they become the prospect. They can smell the sale. They can feel the close coming on.

Customers want to buy. They don't want to be sold.

How do we help somebody buy?

Change the model. Squash out PSC!

Eliminate the word "prospect" from your vocabulary. Stop selling. Never close. You might slam the door on your next customer.

Build relationships with your people by solving their problems instead.

CHAPTER 3

Show, Don't Tell

If you have a business up and running with existing customers, you can develop a personal sales team that will outperform any other marketing push. This sales team can deliver more new customers, more consistently, and with better quality than what you can produce with marketing dollars paid to a third party.

There is a catch to this elite marketing team. It will cost you.

Your marketing team requires care. Invest your time in them. Your team will require top-quality service. You'll have to exceed their expectations all the time, so much so that they will want to hear from you.

The marketing team requires regular follow-up. Check in on them when they don't expect it. Be there for them when they are hurt or when they experience a setback.

Most importantly, you must genuinely care for their welfare. Show them how much you care. Prove to them it's your job to help them succeed. They'll look forward to hearing from you.

Your sales team will make you successful, but it will cost you. It will cost you time, empathy, and authenticity.

Your best sales team is your existing customers. They've already bought from you. You've already helped solve their problems. They keep coming back to you because they depend on you.

Restaurant

Everybody likes to buy. Once they buy, buyers also have a tendency to validate their buying decisions.

Think about the last time you stumbled upon a new restaurant in town. What did you do if the food and service "wowed" you? You told your friends and family about it, especially the foodie types.

"Hey, you've got to check out Pizza for the Heart. It sounds crazy, but they slice the pepperoni so thin it melts into the cheese. They derive the cheese from a fat-free yogurt. And the seaweed crust tastes just like you get in New York. It's a full pizza experience with all the benefits of a health food store."

If your foodie friends trust you, they'll give the restaurant a shot. You've put your reputation on the line. When the restaurant delivers the same quality experience, you're going to look like a hero. But if the restaurant is inconsistent, your friends won't take your word for it the next time.

Maybe you'll try out the next new restaurant a few times before you tell anybody your latest secret.

Similarly, your customers must have enough confidence in you to tell their friends and family about you. This doesn't happen after the first meeting or even as soon as they become a customer. It takes time for customers to join your sales team.

What will it cost you? Your time, your empathy, and your authenticity. If your future sales team is going to tell their friends about you, you must deliver heart-healthy pizza.

From a customer's point of view, it's easy to differentiate yourself from your competition. It's even easier to stand head and shoulders above the rest of the vendors, stores, and service people your customers depend on.

- Show them you genuinely care.
- Follow up with them.
- Ensure they are satisfied.
- Check in on them for no reason.
- Be up-front about your fees.
- Don't ask for referrals.

Your positive reputation will spread throughout your community faster than a heart-healthy pizza shop.

If you have a business up and running, you've probably received referrals, maybe even regularly. Most advisors would say they are always looking for referrals, always asking for referrals.

The methods in this book will take your referrals to another level. With a focus on the customer and a consistent routine, you will exceed customer expectations (not once, but regularly) and create a referral market machine that will take on a life of its own.

As you transition to a referral-focused business, don't immediately abandon your existing market model. Make the change gradually, with purpose. Focus more on customers. Spend less time and money on customer acquisition. The transition will happen incrementally as you elevate your service to where referrals come naturally.

This transition requires authenticity. You must have a genuine desire to help people. Helping people leads to more people to help. If you are just in it to make money, people will see through you, and you will fail.

This transition requires an open mind. Some of the smallest customers refer the biggest customers. You need those who have sampled the pizza to legitimize your ability. You can't do it yourself.

Quality service often impresses the small customers more than it would the big guys. They're not used to being treated as important, so they're more inclined to tell people about you. Small customers can act as sentries for larger customers who may be leery about your services.

Big customers like to hear about experiences from people they trust. They may not think it is safe to enter your office. They may not know you, but when they hear about your high-quality service, they also want you to exceed their expectations. The upside looks good.

A small customer deserves the same respect as the whale of a customer everybody dreams about.

Front Facing

If you've ever been to an election night party, regardless of party affiliation, the political groupies, union bosses, business leaders, and political candidates take part in a schmooze session or political dance. Watching the interactions play out, you will see people looking over each others' shoulders, searching for a better connection.

The politician's playbook looks the same on the campaign trail, especially when cornered by an opinionated constituent with an opposing point of view. They're always looking for the next better person to schmooze.

A friend of mine, Chris, made a run for political office. Having already worked on many candidate campaigns for higher office, he started at the beginning, running for a countywide office.

Long before the election-night party, candidates embark on a summer-long campaign tour of the county, including church festivals, Fourth of July parades, and mini-fundraisers at homes of local supporters.

On a humid night in July, I escorted Chris along with his political hopes around a festival crowd. After passing the cotton candy line and the Tilt-a-Whirl, we found the beer garden to be a good place to engage potential voters. An older man approached in a faded jean jacket and worn-out combat boots. His bloodshot eyes and tangled hair hinted at a hard life.

The wrinkled-faced man didn't look like a voter, much less someone who could help a politician, but he shared his opinion with great enthusiasm. Chris listened intently while droves of potential voters gawked in passing. Our candidate paid full attention to the man's concerns, as though he were the most important person at the festival. When the man finished, he smiled, shook hands, and thanked my friend for listening.

As we watched him blend into the crowd, I asked Chris if he was alright.

He said, "If I'm going to be the county council president, it's my job to understand what matters to the people of this county. That man has the same right to an opinion as the governor."

My friend didn't have to tell the man that he genuinely cared. He showed it.

You can't tell your customers you care. You must show it.

CHAPTER 4

Touch

Developing a referral-based business takes time. There's no question about it. Before you can expect a steady stream of referrals, up your game with your existing customers, and provide trustworthy service. Your clients must trust you.

Good customers are sticky, meaning they stay with you a long time. Great customers are just as sticky. But they not only stay with you, they bring you more good customers.

Around the time I met the hurricaneologists with my friend "Hurricane Pete," I stumbled upon a company dumb enough to hire an inexperienced kid to sell insurance and investments. My sales training was comprised of a single meeting where they asked me to write a list of all my friends and family.

They brainwashed me to see everyone as a client. Soon, everyone I talked to—my aunts, uncles, friends, and even the cashier at Taco Bell—became a potential sale.

I worked my job into every conversation with some comment about how I could save them money on insurance or deliver stellar investment returns. Nobody wanted to talk to me. I failed miserably.

A few months later, a more desperate company offered me an entry-level position. This trust company marketed complicated services to financial advisors for their clients, so the job offered a fantastic opportunity to observe advisors of all skill levels in action.

Some of our advisors cared about their people. More cared about their commissions. The experience opened my eyes to the underbelly of the financial services industry.

It always amazed me to see a person, who seemed to understand so little, be so successful.

One advisor, in particular, caught my attention. Sweet Virginia managed tens of millions of dollars across over fifty trust relationships. Despite her success, she directed all of that money to be invested in a single mutual fund.

I said to my boss, "There's no way this woman knows what she's doing."

He suggested I visit her in person at her Florida office to find out what was going on.

In 1995, we didn't have cell phones, let alone GPS. I was working with a folded map in a farm town somewhere between Orlando and the Gulf of Mexico.

As I pulled my rental car into a shopping strip, the address looked correct, but I only saw a liquor store, a golf cart repair company, and a bill-paying center for the local water department. The shop at the end had no sign, but lots of words painted in blue on the window. It looked like a going out of business sale for a scuba diving store in Kansas.

After a closer look, I realized I was in the right place. The hand-painted words on the window said, "Discount Stocks, Bonds, Mutual Funds." It matched perfectly with the neon lights on the Miller High Life sign at the other end of the strip.

A little bell rang as I poked my head through the door. "I'm here to see Sweet Virginia?"

A woman's voice bellowed from an office within, "About time you got here. Let's get down to business."

I placed a stack of fifty-one investment reviews on her desk. She grabbed the first one. Without looking away from the summary, she asked, "Did you see the yellow church on the way in here after you turned off the highway?"

"Yes."

"This lady paid for the steeple. She loved that church." Sweet Virginia slid the paper aside toward me, then tapped it with her forefinger. Her blue eyes didn't blink. "She left this money to pay for her grandkids' college. When they graduate, the church gets what's left of the money."

She picked up the next review. "This man here was a pillar of the community. It devastated him when dementia took his wife's memory. He funded this trust to guarantee her the best care if something happened to him. Poor guy got hit while riding his bike two years ago. I still visit her at home once a month."

The stories went on. Each account represented a special relationship between Sweet Virginia and her customer—all fifty-one of them.

When we finished the reviews, she pointed across the dusty office at five file cabinets, each four drawers high. "Those cabinets are full of living clients' files who have set up trusts. All of them will become your company's clients within the next twenty years when they die. My responsibility to them is to make sure you do your job."

I asked her how she got new customers.

"I don't sell if that's what you're asking. We have over four hundred customers. Make that four hundred relationships."

She cleared a spot on her desk for her elbows. "New relationships come to me."

"How?"

She leaned halfway across the old desk. "We touch people. First, we spend time with them. Second, we show empathy. And most importantly, we are authentic. We truly care."

I kept listening.

"I like to say we have tea with our customers. Time, empathy, and authenticity—TEA."

Then, Sweet Virginia switched roles from advisor to teacher.

Lesson

She maximized efficiency by having her team split out tasks. Like a doctor, she scheduled in-person appointment hours in blocks. She did the same with outgoing call time, reserving other hours for incoming requests and meeting preparation.

For example, her assistant scheduled nine in-person meetings per week. They reserved Tuesday, Wednesday, and Thursday afternoons for customers. Meeting times were at noon, 1:30 p.m., and 3:00 p.m. This allowed for a one-hour meeting with an extra few minutes if the conversation ran over.

Customers knew that if they scheduled the noon meeting, they would be provided lunch from the local sandwich shop.

Having a limited number of meeting times each week also creates a sense of demand. When a customer realizes your time is scarce, you become more valuable. They respect you as much as you respect them.

Sweet Virginia reserved Monday mornings for client requests. Most money requests and market questions come immediately following the weekend.

Monday afternoons provided quality time to conduct investment reviews and meeting planning for the week.

They called at least five customers per day on Tuesday through Friday mornings. Besides customer contact, her staff used those mornings to file meeting notes, manage their calendar, and respond to routine requests/problems that came up.

With nine meetings and twenty outgoing phone calls, customer service became her number one priority without putting a drag on service.

"If we keep our discipline for fifty weeks out of the year, we'll make a thousand outgoing customer calls." She smiled. "By touching each customer in person or by phone three to six times per year, it's easy to keep your finger on the pulse of your flock. If a customer has a complaint, you will hear about it before it festers into a problem."

Because she contacted her customers so often, her services were on their minds. This led to more business from existing customers and quality referrals with similar needs and personalities as her existing customers.

After I shook her hand, I thanked her for the greatest lesson I had ever received. I sat in the car staring at the painted windows. "Discount Stocks, Bonds, Mutual Funds."

Her people didn't care about the sign on the window or the name of her company. They came to Sweet Virginia because they trusted her.

Sweet Virginia inspired me to become a financial advisor. I decided to model my business after hers.

	Monday	Tuesday	Wednesday	Thursday	Friday
8:00	Client Requests	5+ Customer Calls	5+ Customer Calls	5+ Customer Calls	5+ Customer Calls
8:30					
9:00					
9:30					
10:00					
10:30					
11:00					
11:30					
12:00		In-Person Meeting	In-Person Meeting	In-Person Meeting	
12:30					
1:00	Investment Reviews & Meeting Planning				
1:30		In-Person Meeting	In-Person Meeting	In-Person Meeting	
2:00					
2:30					
3:00		In-Person Meeting	In-Person Meeting	In-Person Meeting	
3:30					
4:00					
4:30					
5:00					

CHAPTER 5

Touching Methodology

Experience teaches that nobody likes to be sold. You can see it in the eyes of friends or acquaintances. Instead of spending so much of your time looking for new customers, spend your time thinking about your existing clients.

Don't see a customer as somebody you closed two years ago. See them as somebody who trusts and depends on you.

Set a goal to spend one hundred percent of your time perfecting a customer-oriented business that grows naturally from referrals.

Escalate your reputation with existing customers.

Communication

Talk to your customers often. Make regular phone calls to check on their well-being three or four times per year. Track and annotate on your customer relationship management (CRM) tool.

All customers deserve at least two phone calls per year and an invitation to meet once per year. Some may defer an in-person meeting if they feel comfortable with your services. Track and annotate the same on your CRM.

Your largest customers deserve an in-person meeting at least twice a year, and no less than annually.

Be available for everyday items five days a week. Set the expectation that you may not respond immediately, but they will hear from you or a member of your team within twenty-four hours.

Customer emergencies can occur twenty-four hours a day. If you give them your personal phone number, set boundaries: emergency only.

Always ask for a customer's emergency contact information in case you lose track of them. Let them know that you will not contact their emergency contact for anything other than to ensure their well-being. You will not discuss their accounts, your services, or your relationship.

Meetings

- Conduct every meeting the same way, always keeping it collegial, not too stuffy.
- Have their name on the screen.
- Begin the meeting with a conversation.
- Review notes from the previous meeting.
- Solve their problems.
- Ask if they are hearing from you enough.

Referrals

Don't ask for referrals. Don't ask for a list of friends or relatives. Your customer came to you for help with personal matters. They didn't come to work for you.

Once you develop a more personal relationship with your customer, you might offer to help others like them.

I have found the following statement gives permission for referrals without instilling a sense of obligation.

"We don't go looking for customers, nor do we ask for referrals. We have plenty of business to keep us busy. We do, however, enjoy working with you. So, if you have colleagues or friends that could use our help, we'd be happy to meet with them, but only if you feel it is a good fit."

Ancillary Services

Always visit the customer in the hospital. Keep the visit short. Bring them something small. I like a word search or crossword puzzle book. A couple of scratch-off lottery tickets will take their mind away from the current situation.

Always attend a funeral, whether it's for a family member or the customer themselves. Live by it. If you don't know the rest of the family, get there early. I always talk to the customer or spouse, but sometimes politely make my way around other family members who wouldn't know me.

If anything reminds you of a customer, call them within twenty-four hours. Let them know you were thinking of them and why. Chances are, they will have been thinking of you or have something to ask you. Depending on how the conversation goes, this could count as a check-in phone call tracked on your CRM.

Send articles of interest to your customers via email or snail mail. When you send them, do not use them as a Trojan horse to set up meetings, business, or product. Remember, personal mail is memorable, especially if you avoid PSC. No selling.

The most forward sales line you should use is, "Please don't hesitate to call if there is anything I can help you with."

Build customer contact into your daily routine. Always use your CRM to track phone and in-person contacts.

Be Efficient

As your business grows, managing so many contacts can become a challenge.

When I started in business, my customers dictated my calendar. When a customer called, I asked when they wanted to come in. If they said 7:30 a.m., I'd meet them for coffee. Lunch? No problem. They want to meet after hours? No problem. I'd rearrange my schedule. I was so happy to have the appointment that I agreed to whatever time they wanted.

Having a conversation with a friend or loved one proves challenging if you are also watching an Instagram Reel of a puppy that can play the harmonica. It's impossible to pay attention to both. Usually, it's the conversation that suffers. Over time, it could even damage the relationship.

It's the same with business. You can't be responding to phone calls or processing distribution requests while preparing for the next meeting that starts in ten minutes.

As the business grew, my flexibility became a detriment to our efficiency. It detracted from our ability to serve the client in the manner they deserved.

Haphazard meeting times chopped up the day. Our administrative tasks, meeting preparation, and routine calls took a back seat to face time with the customer.

If your business is going to execute at a high level, the behind-the-scenes work is just as important as face time with customers. If you try to accomplish both, you'll have less success—like a serious conversation being interrupted by a puppy playing the harmonica.

You can't do both at the same time. It's just as hard to switch from busy work to customer satisfaction. Changing hats and shifting gears among investment research, compliance, and customer face time diminished the quality of our work.

Have scheduled meeting times. Separate them from daily work.

Small Touches

Remember how Sweet Virginia systematized the touch.

Call at least five customers per day on Tuesday through Friday mornings.

Set standard appointment times on specific days. Set a goal to see nine people per week.

Besides customer contact, use your nonmeeting times to scan meeting notes, manage your CRM, and respond to routine requests/problems that come up.

With nine meetings and twenty outgoing phone calls, customer service naturally becomes the number one priority without putting a drag on service.

Use Sweet Virginia's simple magic. With a thousand outgoing customer calls and 450 meetings, your people will know how much you care. You won't have to tell them. That kind of customer service lays the foundation for referrals from satisfied customers.

If you have out-of-town customers, make it a point to see them in person once a year. We block out five weeks a year for travel, with visits to Florida during the winter months. In these cases, we attempt to string a few meetings together by region. Acknowledging that we may only see three people a week when traveling and another nine per week when in the office, we have the capability of 425 face-to-face meetings per year.

Front Facing

After a new advisor completed his second week of work, I tasked him with calling five customers. Before he picked up the phone, we reviewed each customer's history, personal situation, and investments. Our young advisor had two directives: to check with each customer on their well-being and to ask if they needed anything.

Having plenty of customer-facing experience, he jumped at the opportunity. He understood not to discuss money or product. His only goal was to make sure they were happy.

An hour later, a ghost-like figure appeared in my doorway. He leaned his shoulder against the doorframe. Stunned and out of breath, he glared at me as if a horn was growing from my forehead. I thought he might quit.

"What's wrong?"

"I've called hundreds of clients for financial advisors, even more when I worked at the big bank. None of those people wanted to hear from me."

I stood up, concerned that something negative had happened.

"But today, every person I called was happy to hear from me. They all said to tell you 'Hello.' It was amazing."

Customers enjoy hearing from you, especially when you are acting in their interests.

CHAPTER 6

First Impression

The first five chapters of this book focus on developing your existing practice into one that delivers exceptional customer service. When you exceed your customers' expectations all the time, they will become comfortable telling friends and family about how great you are.

As you journey down the referral road, it may help to compare the process to dating. In order to develop a committed relationship with a complete stranger, you must navigate through the first impression, then the blind date before your customer becomes committed to your service.

Each stage incrementally builds trust between you and your "referee" until they become a loyal customer.

A referral is the greatest compliment from your customers. They are happy with your service. If you deliver quality service or a great product, you're inevitably going to receive referrals.

Before you can grow a relationship, you must plant the first seed with a good first impression.

When a customer relationship has matured to one of complete trust, your customer may take on a new role as referrer. This can be a big risk for the referrer because it could jeopardize their relationship with the person they are referring to you.

They trust you, so they expect you to deliver the same experience to their friend or colleague, the referee. Now you have a new responsibility to your customer, the referrer. It's your job to make them a hero by delivering outstanding service to the referee.

Let's talk about what can happen.

After the initial referral, when your customer brags to their friend or colleague (the referee) about you, it's up to you to schedule the first meeting. To secure an initial meeting, you must make a memorable *first impression*, a critical stepping stone on the road to referrals.

Remember the hurricaneologists. Don't chase. Let them choose.

Types Of Initial Referrals

There are a few different types of referrals:

- *The soft referral.* Your customer calls and says, "I told referee about you. She really needs your help. Here's her phone number." Ask your customer to have the referee reach out to you directly, or ask your customer to send an introductory email.
- *The introductory email.* The referrer sends a group email to introduce the referee to you. Reply to all, inviting the referee to reach out to you via phone. When the referee reaches out, follow the script below.
- *The surprise.* The referee calls to schedule a meeting before your referrer lets you know. This is the best thing that can happen; the referee has chosen you. Be ready with your own version of the script below.

In all three situations, you want to speak with them, so they can hear the authenticity in your voice.

In all three situations, your only goal is to schedule the first meeting, the blind date.

Most likely, experience has conditioned the referee to expect you to be salesy. They expect to feel like a prospect. They expect you to sound sleazy.

Your instinct will be to tell them what you can do. Don't. Break the PSC mold. Forget prospecting, stop selling, and never be closing. You will differentiate yourself immediately. Discipline and consistency are the keys to success.

Script

1. Thank the referee for calling.
2. Acknowledge your customer (the referrer) who introduced the two of you.
3. Focus the conversation on the referee.
4. Set the expectations for the first meeting. Invite the referee to come into the office to interview you to make sure it's a good fit—no obligation, no costs.
5. Invite them to provide you any documents that will give a perspective of their current situation or documents they might want you to review. For example: accountants' tax returns, financial advisors' statements, and lawyers' will, power of attorney and health care directive.
6. Don't talk about your process or product.
7. Show them you are busy by scheduling an appointment in your office for a week to ten days out.

Front Facing

Here's a slighty different take on a business to business referral.

A colleague of mine provides attorneys with ancillary services such as personal trusteeship or registered agency. He asked for advice on how to build a bigger book of customers. I offered to reach out to a trusted attorney to talk up my colleague's services.

Being the referrer, I highlighted his qualifications, how long I've known him, and how much I trust him. Without hesitating, the attorney asked me to have him call her. Five minutes later, I was on the phone to give him the good news.

The next day, I checked in with him. He hadn't connected with her because he was stuck drafting an email that would tell her everything he could do without bragging.

I told him to stop writing.

The referee, my attorney friend, already had a positive impression of him because I told her how great he was. She didn't need, nor would she want, to hear it again, especially from him.

All he had to do was write a two-sentence email to schedule a meeting over coffee. If he did any more than that, he would look sleazy, I mean salesy. He wasn't trying to sell something. He was developing a professional relationship.

Take one step at a time. Make the first impression. That's where you plant the seed for the relationship. Think of the process as setting up a blind date. Get the blind date.

CHAPTER 7

Blind Date

After the initial referral and a quality first impression, the referee will agree to a face-to-face meeting. Professionally speaking, the blind date is the first meeting between the referral and the professional.

If you have followed the proper steps, the referee:

- Already knows you have a good reputation
- Already knows something about your background
- Already suspects you are authentic because there was no hint of PSC; they are hoping for something special.

Now it's time to exceed expectations.

No matter how great your first impression, your referee will still feel some intimidation as they approach your meeting. Ease their concerns by maintaining professionalism combined with a welcome-home atmosphere.

Make them feel like it's a private meeting at their doctor's office—and the doctor is a trusted friend.

Meeting Preparation

Don't call the referee in advance to remind them of the meeting. This seems pushy and makes them feel like a prospect. Show professionalism. Avoid PSC.

Have a conference room available. Avoid meeting in your office if possible. The conference room makes for a more neutral meeting place.

Have a simple snack on the table. It can be cookies (everybody loves Girl Scout Cookies if in season), snack-size candy bars, or mints.

Have two cold bottles each of water and sparkling water on the table within reach of the referee.

Have a pen resting on a single sheet of blank copy paper in the middle of the table. This isn't for notes, but available for drawing a picture to simplify complicated subjects. You may also need the paper at the end of the meeting when you don't ask for the sale.

Have a conversation piece or a framed quote on the side table. I always keep an electric train engine on the side table. To the right of the train, a framed four-square comic from *Peanuts* depicts Linus teaching Charlie Brown about happiness.

If the referee hasn't arrived within fifteen minutes of the scheduled meeting time, you can call them. Ask if they had trouble finding the office. Most likely, they forgot about the meeting.

Referee Arrival

Have your assistant offer coffee, water, or sparkling water while they wait. If they arrive early, don't rush out to meet them. Finish your current call, task, or meeting. You may start the meeting early if it's convenient for you. Whatever you do, the latest you should start is on time.

I prefer to schedule a break between meetings, so customers don't run into each other. It maintains their privacy.

Greet them in the waiting room and escort them to the meeting room. Thank them for taking the time to meet with you.

Offer the referee the seat at the head of the table with you sitting to their side. Do not sit across from them. The meeting should feel cooperative.

The Blind Date Do's

After the referee sits down and is comfortable, give them control of the meeting. Ask them where they would like to start. Usually, they'll open the discussion with what's bothering them.

Acknowledge the referrer, your customer, who introduced you. Ask them what they know about your background. Offer to discuss your background further if necessary. Keep it short. Only touch on key points that make you a pro. The focus should be on the customer.

Treat the meeting like a first date. Show genuine interest. Ask about family, hobbies, career, or industry. View the referee as a human being who needs help with a problem. Remember to forget PSC. Avoid assumptions.

Keep the conversation loose. The meeting should feel natural for both parties.

Review any paperwork they bring along and ask pertinent questions.

Blind Date Don'ts

Don't tell them everything you know. You have nothing to prove. The referrer already told them you are great, *and* the referee showed up for the blind date. Remember the acronym WAIT, which stands for "Why am I talking?" Let them talk.

Don't take notes. It can be intimidating in the first meeting. Notes are also presumptive, especially if the referee is unsure whether they will work with you.

Don't have a client data sheet to fill out. It's intimidating, presumptive, and corporate. You'll have time to get to know each other if the relationship proceeds.

Be the airline pilot. Let them know where you will take them, but don't discuss the fuel or the flight plan. Offer a vision for the future, but don't tell them how you are going to solve their problem.

Wrapping Up The Blind Date

Discuss your fees and any other costs the customer may incur.

Ask them how they feel about what they've heard so far.

Offer to let them leave personal information on the blank copy paper for you to complete the account-opening paperwork, but only if they choose to come back. Let them know you will shred the information if they decide not to come back.

Suggest they think it over before deciding to work with you. Maybe discuss it with a significant other.

Only schedule the next meeting if they request it.

Afterward

Jot down a few notes. Add them to a temporary file with whatever information they leave behind for a more thorough review.

Add the referee name to your CRM and schedule a follow-up ten days in advance. If the meeting went well, this should prove redundant because they will probably call before that.

Within twenty-four hours, mail a handwritten thank-you note in a handwritten envelope with the latest commemorative stamp. Nobody gets snail mail like this anymore. It's memorable. *Do not include your card.* They know who you are and have your number.

Do not call them for at least ten days.

Remember the law of the hurricaneologists.

Don't chase. Let them choose.

Front Facing

I worked with a customer whom I'll call Lori, who was suffering through a divorce. I helped her understand a potential process to split up the assets. It made so much sense to her that she asked me to meet with her future ex-husband to help work things out.

I only agreed to meet with him on one condition: He had to schedule the meeting. Let them choose. And he did, but he scheduled the meeting after business hours.

My staff had left for the evening when I heard pounding coming from the lobby. As I opened the door, I found a high-and-tight crew cut and a scowl on a retired Marine that could have scared the Germans away from Normandy Beach.

His handshake almost broke my hand. When I told him I was a Navy veteran, he said, "That's all right, you can shine my boots on the way out."

He sat down, cracked open a club soda, then glared at me.

"I lost half my Marine Corps pension to my first ex-wife. I earned what's left of it before I met Lori. I don't want to lose the other half to her."

"Sounds reasonable," I said, then explained I was there to help them both. Whatever I said to her, I would also discuss with him. And vice versa.

The tension evaporated. Within minutes, he listed everything they owned. I drew a circle, then cut it into proportionate slices, showing the size of each of their assets.

I put the pension on his side of the circle, then penciled in her smaller pension and a 401(k) on the other. Cars, furniture, house, savings. It all went into the circle. Then

I drew a line down the middle, showing how they could each walk away with half.

"When can all three of us meet to hash this out?"

At the joint meeting, they agreed on everything, except for who would get custody of the dog.

A few months later, Lori was still my customer. Then, to my surprise, the marine hired me. He went from referee to customer. I never shined his boots, nor did I ask him for his business. By listening, I turned a bad situation into two customers who sent me more referrals.

CHAPTER 8

Pitch Slapped

A few years back, an out-of-state attorney sent us an unsolicited referral. His client requested information regarding charitable planning. One of my younger associates (I'll call him Salesy Sam) received the call, then quickly took his own initiative.

In hindsight, I wish he hadn't, because we "pitch slapped" her.

Here's what happened.

Within minutes of the attorney referral, Salesy Sam called Pam Prospect. (I use the word prospect because that's how Sam treated her.) The referee didn't return his call. I'm not sure exactly what he said, but I have a good idea. An hour after leaving a voicemail, Salesy Sam delivered his message a second time, via follow-up email:

Pam,

I called earlier after connecting with your attorney, Eddie Embarrassed. Eddie provided your contact information and asked that we reach out for an introduction [sic] meeting. I have copied the leader here in our local office in Wilmington, Delaware, Paul Dorsey.

Not only are we local, but we also specialize in high-net-worth and ultra-high-net-worth family foundations locally. We work with Eddie Embarrassed all the time. We are an extension of his firm's white glove service.

Our assistant will send our team's availability shortly. She will provide a handful of dates/times we can meet over the next two to three weeks.

Sincerely,
Salesy Sam

Sam called Pam again the next day. When she didn't answer, he left a second message. He waited less than a day before following up with another email.

Sam had great initiative, but sometimes initiative kills sales. Pam Prospect never called, never emailed. Not even a smoke signal.

Poor Pam received four contacts in four days from an unknown advisor. Talk about being pitch slapped.

When I found out what happened, I was more embarrassed for the attorney than for myself. I called to apologize. The conversation didn't go well.

"Dorsey! What the hell were you thinking?"

I had no words.

"I referred my friend Pam to you because she had basic questions I thought you could answer. If it turned into a relationship for you, great. Now she thinks I promised you a high-net-worth client."

He caught his breath and continued, "Then she asked me the difference between high-net-worth and ultra-high-net-worth. And worse, she questioned my integrity."

I let him vent some more, then took the blame and apologized. We never received another referral from him.

A few months later, Salesy Sam moved on from our company. We never heard from him again, either. Maybe he's selling cars.

Lessons

Building an ounce of trust will impress a potential customer way more than a pound of professional pontification. Never tell a potential customer what you can do for them before you've earned their trust.

Don't brag about your existing customers. It's presumptive. The potential customer may have nothing in common with them.

Keep the referrer (in this case, the attorney) in the loop during the entire referral process.

Let them choose you. Only contact a potential customer after they contact you.

Don't make multiple contacts. It associates you with the rest of your competition.

Don't make multiple contacts. You look desperate and unprofessional.

Avoid formalities in your conversation and voicemail. Introducing the advisor as a "leader" is a form of corporate speak. It kills new business.

Avoid industry language. "High-net-worth" and "ultra-high-net-worth individuals," along with "white-glove treatment," sound like big-company television advertisements and corporate speak. Customers have relationships with people, not big companies.

Be yourself. Build the relationship, not the sale.

CHAPTER 9

Shine A Light

When shopping in a big box store like Target or Home Depot, shoppers can often hear a bird chirping from the rafters. The bird's song sounds more like desperation, much different from the melody you might hear from the same bird outside your bedroom window as morning breaks.

One December evening, I stepped out of my front door for some fresh air. I didn't see a sparrow foraging in the garden off to the right. Terrified, the sparrow flew directly at me, chirping in fear.

As I ducked, my newfound friend flew through the open door and into the foyer. By the time I turned around, the little guy had found his way to the highest and safest spot, a curtain rod in the living room.

I tried in vain to coax him back to the front door with a broom. I talked to the little bird as it hopped from side to side, bobbing its head above the curtains. My daughters found the whole situation entertaining. Their grandmother watched from the safety of the second floor stairway.

The dance between the bird and me went on for about half an hour. The bird and I had the same goal, but I couldn't communicate how I wanted to help him. He felt safe on the curtain rod, wanting nothing to do with getting back to the foyer where an open door and freedom waited.

Then, by accident, my oldest daughter hit the light switch, and the living room went dark.

The bird whizzed over our heads to the light atop the stairway.

"Now, we'll never get him out," I said, thinking of those poor birds trapped in the Home Depot.

"He's looking for a light," said my older daughter.

I shuffled through the kitchen junk drawer for a flashlight.

"You know, you have one of those on your phone," scoffed daughter #2.

After we shut the lights out on the ground floor, daughter #2 handed the flashlight to her grandmother.

"Open the front door all the way," she told me. "Mimi, shine the light down here."

A beam lit up the wall at the bottom of the steps. We heard the bird's wings flutter as it descended the steps toward the circle of light on the wall.

"Now show him the door!"

Mimi led the bird by shining the light on the open door. The bird flew to safety, and we breathed a sigh of relief.

Show Them The Light

Potential customers don't always understand the benefits of your service. They've often done the work themselves. Investors may not need financial advice until they become empty-nesters, and they're able to save more money. Married couples may have never thought about hiring an attorney until the subject of divorce or estate planning arises. Accountants may seem out of reach until a side gig generates more cash than the salary earned from a W-2 job.

In each of the above cases, potential customers may not understand the value of personal services.

The sparrow in the living room wouldn't have found its way back to safety without our help.

But we couldn't tell the bird, "We're here to help you find the door."

We could yell as much as we could to tell the bird to go out the door, but it wouldn't budge.

Our bird understood two things: height and light.

In an unknown space, a bird naturally flies to the highest point. Height represents safety, and for good reason. The bird can look down and see me if I try to climb up to grab him. He would then hop to another curtain rod.

Also, for the bird, I learned that light represents safety. When my daughter shut off the light, the bird flew toward a dimmer light in a more precarious location. Upstairs was higher, but it offered less of an escape to freedom.

The bird couldn't rationalize that it was in a different environment, an environment with different rules than the natural environment outside.

We genuinely wanted to avoid having a bird as a housemate, but we had no way to earn its trust. We only understood the bird's instincts when it flew toward the dimmer light.

The light simplified a complex problem for us humans and the bird. Within seconds, the sparrow's trauma ended for both us and the bird, with no injuries.

Your customers understand two things: their problem and the past. People who have life changes often find themselves in new environments. Their instinct to act is based on outdated experiences. They don't know that acting as they have in the past can cause them more harm.

A risk-averse investor who inherits significant assets may leave them in the same stocks their grandfather had forgotten about twenty years prior.

An ex-husband or ex-wife who signs off on a divorce settlement just to be free could jeopardize their economic future or retirement. Proper representation from an attorney would help them make a well-rounded decision.

When you build trust with a potential customer, they will begin to understand how you can help them. They will see your value. Show them the light.

CHAPTER 10

Dating

On the blind date, the referee will have acted as their own "referee." Picture them wearing a black-and-white striped shirt, deciding if you caught the ball or fumbled it before you stepped on the out-of-bounds line.

If you listened with genuine concern, disclosed your fees with confidence, and sent a handwritten thank-you note with a commemorative stamp, you will have a 95 percent chance of hearing from them before you follow up.

When you receive the call for a second meeting, it indicates that they are interested in a relationship. They want to go steady. Clearly, they want to work with you. And you didn't chase them. They chose you. This is the foundation for a long-term relationship.

During the scheduling call, have your assistant schedule them at their preferred time during your office hours. Consider offering their choice of hoagies or other sandwiches if they schedule a lunch meeting. Some people feel more comfortable meeting over lunch. A few will decline lunch, preferring to keep the business meeting more formal.

As you prepare for the second meeting, consistency is key. Don't change your personality or approach. Forget any training you've had in PSC. Don't prospect. Don't sell. Don't close. They are human beings looking for help, like a patient needs a doctor.

Meeting Preparation

- Have refreshments/lunch on the table with plates and cold drinks.
- Have short notes from your initial meeting.
- Have a formal note page with their name and date typed/printed at the top of the page. List generic agenda items with sufficient space to take notes under each topic.
- Be completely prepared.
- If you have a big screen on the wall for information sharing, have their name on the screen. If you don't have a big screen on the wall, get one. It's much better than using your computer screen. It also puts

you on the same side of the table as the customer. You are looking at the same screen at the same time.

- Have relevant documents, new account forms, account lists, and tax returns available on the screen or in a folder.
- Review all of your forms for accuracy: name spelling, social security, and birthdates. Customers care if you have them correctly identified.

Remember, the referee has returned because they know you are a professional. They want your help in problem-solving or decision-making. Let them be the main character in the meeting. Avoid all veiled attempts at sales. Give them an active part in the conversation.

WAIT. Stay true to the question, "Why am I talking?"

Until now, you've avoided PSC. Did I mention the fourth dirty word?

Product.

Never use the word *product.* Erase it from your vocabulary. Professional advisors deliver a service. They use/deliver/provide certain investments to provide the service, but they are not selling a product. They solve problems.

Meeting Conduct

- Thank them for coming in for a second meeting. Their return is the greatest compliment they can offer.

- Ask them where they want to start. If it's a lunch meeting, pass the sandwiches around first. This creates a cooperative atmosphere. It helps them let their guard down from any expectations of a hidden PSC.

- Acknowledge their issue.

- Be serious, but not too serious. Inject topics such as current events, people in common, or short stories to keep the meeting flowing. It also helps you to get to know them and them to know you.

- Discuss the subject on the customer's level. Don't confuse them by trying to impress them with industry terms. If you raise a complex subject, watch their eyes to ensure they understand. Be quick to simplify, tell a story, or use metaphors if necessary.

- Do not talk about yourself. Customers listen to the proverbial radio station, WIIFM. They want to know, "What's in it for me?" You are there to play their tune. The doctor doesn't talk about their own ailments. They help their patients with their ailments.

- Don't overpromise. Always tell the truth.

- Walk them through any forms, stopping at critical fields like social security number and birthday.

End Of Meeting

- Review notes from today's meeting. Read them out loud. Have them sign or initial the bottom of the note page. Offer a copy if they want one. Let them know you will review those notes at the start of the next meeting.
- Don't ask for referrals. Don't suggest that you are happy to help their friends. This is only the second date. You're not that intimate yet.
- Set expectations of what will happen over the next thirty days.
- Schedule a follow-up meeting within thirty to forty-five days to review their new account, changes, taxes, etc.
- Set long-term expectations. How often will they hear from you and in what manner? Offer one meeting a year, unless they require more attention, and quarterly phone calls.
- Ask them if there is anything else they want to discuss. Ask them if they feel comfortable.

- Walk them to the door and hand them your business card from the stack at the front desk. Jot down your cell phone number on the back of the card, letting them know it's only for emergencies. Then thank them for their confidence in you.

After The Meeting

- Add check boxes to action items on the note page. Use these as a checklist (including next meeting) to add to your CRM.

- Set up an action item for a follow-up call to the new customer (not referee) the week before the next meeting.

Front Facing

In researching this book, I asked a long-time customer what drew her to me as a financial advisor. Without hesitation, she said, "It felt like family when we started working together. You didn't advertise. You didn't sell. I met your friends, family, and other clients at your customer appreciation dinners. And they were truly appreciation dinners. No selling. Hell, I knew about your wife and your kids. Even your dog."

Replace prospecting, selling, and closing with genuine concern for your people. Your customers will develop a sense of trust in you that becomes contagious.

CHAPTER 11

Be A Good Dog

From the very beginning, I grew up with a fear of dogs. I didn't always understand them. We weren't a dog family. I had allergies. If I spent time in a friend's house who had a lab, the lab could sense my fear. He'd jump on me, lick my hands and face, then lean on his hind legs and bark at me. Somehow, the lab knew. Then after fifteen minutes, I'd have to leave the house, wheezing with a severe asthma attack.

In that same light, I don't trust salespeople.

After my wife and I first married, the local newspaper published the details of our wedding, complete with pictures of the smiling bride and groom. In the ensuing weeks, our phone rang incessantly with sales calls from strangers. One gentleman passed the first impression test and successfully set up an appointment in our home. He promised to help us buy quality meat at wholesale prices and offered a no-obligation meeting. If we didn't buy, he would leave us a sirloin steak so we would know what we were missing.

After the initial hello, the meeting went downhill like a rocket sled on rails. If the bait was a free two-inch-thick sirloin steak, the switch was a brand-new freezer. Before pricing out a dozen hot dogs, he offered us a deal on a freezer to store the monthly meat delivery. We couldn't afford a $500 refrigerator, let alone a $2,000 freezer. Not a problem, he said. His company could finance it for us at a 12 percent interest rate. Talk about being pitch slapped.

We politely declined and slowly led the sleazy Mr. Salesy to the door. He stormed out, then drove away with wheels squealing.

Michele looked at me and said, "All that stress and he didn't even leave the steak."

Bad dog.

Soon after that, a different salesperson knocked on our door, but we didn't see him at first. At three feet tall, the little boy might have been eight years old. With disheveled hair and torn jeans, he wore shoes a few sizes too big. But what drew our attention was the puppy he was carrying on his side like a football.

Michele opened the storm door. Before she could ask his name, he said, "My mom says if I don't find a home for this dog, I have to leave it in the park."

She knelt down to the boy's level. He continued. "Would you buy it for five dollars?"

We paid the five bucks, then quietly agreed the dog would only stay a day, long enough for us to find her a home. Being jet black, we named her Jetta. Giving her a name was a mistake.

That one-day stay turned into a lifetime. And those five bucks were the most expensive five dollars we ever spent. A few years later, Jetta helped welcome our firstborn to the family. Four years later, her excitement didn't change when our second born arrived. Our kids grew up with her.

Jetta's not with us anymore, but a chance knock on our door changed how I felt about dogs. Thirty years later, every time I walk into the laundry room and see her ashes in her little box, I think of how much that little black mutt meant to our family.

Good dog.

The human-dog relationship is one of the most trusted and enduring relationships a person can have. It's rooted in a mix of psychology and mutual benefit. Think about your dog.

Dogs are loyal. They create a strong emotional attachment.

Dogs understand us. They help people with post-traumatic stress disorder (PTSD), anxiety, and depression. They sense distress and respond compassionately.

Dogs protect us. They warn us of intruders or danger. They make us feel safe.

And in return, we treat dogs as members of the family. We take care of our dogs.

There's no bad dog in this world. Some dogs have been abused or improperly trained. They often give off bad vibes, hurting the dog community's reputation like the meat guy who tried to sell us a refrigerator. He hadn't learned the basics of customer service.

Then there are good dogs. Like your dog. Or my dog. Or Jetta. Good dogs are genuine and authentic. You can trust them.

Remember that little boy who sold us our favorite mutt? Even though he tried to make a buck, he told us the truth. I'm sure that little person grew up to be a great salesperson. And that's not the point.

If you want a successful referral business, learn from your dog.

Be loyal to your customer. Create strong, emotional attachments.

Understand your customer. Know when the world is crashing down on them. Know when they are celebrating success. Respond compassionately, either way.

Protect your customers. Give them a feeling of safety from what they don't understand or can't do.

When you become an extended member of your customer's family, you become their go-to person when they need somebody they can trust. They'll take care of you with referrals.

Be a good dog.

CHAPTER 12

Strengthen The Chain

No matter how hard you try, you will occasionally have a breakdown in service. You or your staff will miss your high standard target. If customers feel it, they may refer less business.

For example, if somebody calls, but you don't get the message, they won't receive the return call they expect. By the time you hear about it, your customer's vexation has already been brewing long enough to have frustrated them. You must act as soon as possible.

Get a complete understanding of what happened, then pick up the phone. Acknowledge the mistake and apologize. Then make up for it in a way that leaves the customer feeling better than before the mistake was made.

There's an old saying about links in a chain. If a link weakens or breaks, it puts the chain at risk. But when a welder repairs the link, it makes the link stronger than the rest of the chain's links. You can create a more loyal customer after a letdown or mistake by making them feel whole, proving that the mistake was just an isolated incident. You want them to know that nothing has changed your company standards.

Twenty years ago, we started going to a pizza chain because their rosemary and garlic wings tasted like my Italian grandmother's chicken. They were good-sized, juicy, and flavorful. I brought all my wholesalers to lunch there. Everybody loved them.

One time, we received an order of overcooked wings. The dried-out skin cracked like plastic, and the meat tasted like newspaper. Embarrassed for my guest, I swore I'd never go back. After a few days, my wife suggested I talk to the manager.

I gave the restaurant another chance. Before ordering my pizza, I let the manager know how disappointed I had been with the wings. She apologized and said she wished she had known. As we waited for the pizza, she surprised us with twenty wings, then picked up our entire meal with a smile and another sincere apology.

A weak link in the chain suddenly became stronger. We've been loyal to the restaurant ever since, introducing new people to their wings for twenty years.

So, if someone complains about the service, it's nothing personal. It means you treated them in a way that wasn't up to their expectations. Make it right. It strengthens the bond.

CHAPTER 13

Respect Generates Referrals

When my wife and I became engaged, she was still living at home. I was renting a room at a friend's house. We had big dreams of paying for a wedding and buying our first house in the same year.

As a young twenty-something couple, we didn't know any Realtors.

So we went on open house tours every weekend.

With each house, we ran into a new real estate agent. Each one seemed to look for new clients as much, if not more, than trying to sell the house. Once they learned they were dealing with a couple of soon-to-be newlyweds who were approved for a mortgage, they pounced. Like walking into the car dealer, we felt like deer being stalked by a hunter.

Now this was the early 1990s, back before the Earth cooled. The internet was still in diapers, so we had little information on the housing market. If we were going to find a house before the wedding, we needed a Realtor.

Time became of the essence. One Sunday, we stumbled upon an open house on the corner across from the church where we were to be married. The home had a huge front porch with roll-out windows. It wasn't really attractive to either of us.

"Let's check out the price," said my wife. "At least it's close to my parents."

The showing real estate agent sat alone at a desk in the living room. Maybe we missed the crowd.

She welcomed us with pleasantries, pointed out the recently updated kitchen, and mentioned some drawbacks with an older electrical system. Then she invited us to tour the house on our own.

When we finished our tour, she asked us to sign the book and leave feedback for the sellers. She offered her card. "Call me if you have questions."

As we drove away, we knew the house wasn't for us, but agreed there was something about the Realtor. She didn't sell. We were more comfortable without somebody watching over our shoulders. For the first time in our search for a home, we didn't feel like hunted deer.

A few days later, my wife received a personally addressed envelope in the mail, a note from the realtor. She thanked us for stopping in, then offered her phone number if there was anything she could do to help us.

That Sunday, we went on our regular open house tour. After being accosted by two more real estate agents, we retreated to her parents' home to make sandwiches. On the way, we passed a house across the street from my high school that had been for sale for months.

My wife asked, "Why don't we ask our no-pressure realtor to show us that high school house we drive by three times a day?"

The rest is history.

Three months later, my groomsmen met at our new house across from the high school for the bachelor party. I told them about how we found the house.

Nobody referred us to the no-pressure realtor, but she was the perfect example of a person who created her own referral. It's very simple. She didn't treat us as prospects, a sale, or a close. She developed our trust by showing she cared.

She didn't chase us. We chose her because she showed genuine concern.

CHAPTER 14

Build It Yourself

When I started in business, an accountant friend of mine invited me to a morning networking group. What better way to get the word out about what I do?

At the informational breakfast, I learned a few things. It cost $800 per year to be a member. The membership was exclusive to one member per business line; they only allowed one attorney, one carpet cleaner, or one clown in the group. This avoided inter-network competition. The group expected fellow members to use only other members of the group, regardless of the quality of work. They also required members to give referral preference to other members of the group, regardless of the quality of work.

They invited new members based on a relationship or reputation with one person in the group. The only thing each person had in common was they were the sole line of their business in the group. It felt like a forced fraternity relationship with a group of friends I never met before.

My intuition told me to pass on the $800 and my new friends. But the referral concept intrigued me.

I soon realized I could build a network of people I trusted and didn't have to pay for it.

Front Facing

Early on in my career, a customer bragged to me about how much attention she received from her accountant. I asked her to tell the accountant about me, then made my first impression by setting up a professional blind date.

We interviewed each other over lunch. She told war stories about unnamed IRA beneficiaries. I brought up a postal carrier who neglected to file his tax return for five years, despite multiple tax refunds waiting for him. That accountant became a routine referral for our customers who needed help with their taxes.

At one time, our office worked with three attorneys, that is, until we found the right fit. She listened to her customers, allowed input from their financial advisor, and, most importantly, spoke in terms that laypeople could understand. She treated our customers the way we wanted to be treated. And her fees were more reasonable than lawyers who couldn't communicate with nonlawyer types.

One day, an acquaintance recognized me in line at Dunkin' Donuts. His daughter played in the same softball league as my girls. We talked about the parents we knew in common. Joe didn't mention that he was a roof guy until I asked as we left the donut shop. Don't chase. Let them choose.

I shook his hand and added him to my referral database.

Soon, a customer called the office in tears. A roofer she found online recommended a new roof to the tune of $30,000. I suggested she call Joe for a second opinion. After he inspected the roof, the ecstatic client left a message, "Joe says my roof has another ten years left. He told me to spend the money on my broken HVAC system. You don't know how relieved I am."

Over the years, we've referred over twenty clients who were concerned about the integrity of their roof. He's only installed three roofs. That's a referral you can trust.

After herniating a disc, pain radiated down from my right shoulder to my thumb. A back surgeon suggested I try physical therapy or chiropractic care before giving in to the knife. Physical therapy failed, so I tried a chiropractor who lived up the street from my mother and advertised heavily.

This guy zapped me with electric therapy, then forced my right knee into my left shoulder like a toy doll. Barely able to walk to the car, I swore off chiropractors.

My right arm remained in pain. Weeks later, a childhood friend referred me to chiropractor #2. I told him he was crazy for using a chiropractor. Then chiropractor #2 called me to say I should never leave a chiropractor in more pain than when I went in. He invited me to interview him in person to understand his simple technique.

A few visits later, a simple crack (he hates that term) of the neck sent a shiver down my right arm, alleviating all pain. Twenty years later, I still visit him every week. He receives multiple referrals from me each year. In return, he has saved many friends and clients from surgery.

Each of these people serves as an arrow I keep in my "service quiver" for my existing customers. There are many others. We trust our referrals to deliver a quality product or service. The only thing we expect in return is that they take care of our clients.

We have a customer who calls me when she needs somebody to work on her house or when she has a friend in need. When we answer the phone, she doesn't say hello. She says, "Dorsey's gotta guy." If we don't have somebody she needs, we find somebody who knows somebody who can help. Then we add another arrow to our quiver.

Build Your Own Referral Network

Give more referrals than you receive.

Expect nothing in return except good service. You are in it for your customer, not to get paid back. If they don't refer to you, don't take it personally.

Follow up with both parties involved in the referral. Ensure the referee and the referral are satisfied.

Build relationships with trusted people who work tangentially to your industry: lawyers, accountants, roofers, window installers, siding companies, contractors, surgeons, and family doctors.

Only refer high-quality professionals. Don't refer somebody just because they sent a customer to you. This can and will jeopardize your reputation. Offer the referral if you know they can provide the exceptional service that your customers expect.

Refer your customers to each other. We have a second-generation customer whom we met while helping his mother find a retirement home. He manages a large auto body shop. When we received a call from another customer whose sixteen-year-old had a fender bender, we made the connection. One customer becomes the referral. The other becomes a referee again. Here, we called the body shop manager before the referee made contact. Avoid surprises with either party.

Only introduce customers to providers. Don't discuss cost or pricing. Just make a solid connection that the referee can trust.

Stay in touch with your referral sources. If your calendar gets light, meet referral sources you haven't seen recently for coffee or lunch. Let them know what's going on in your industry. More importantly, ask about their business. Then shut up and "WAIT." Remember the acronym for "Why am I talking?"

I recently had a friend in the floor industry text me for breakfast. He texted, "Why don't we make it a point to bump into each other at breakfast?" What a great invitation. We met with no expectations except to catch up. Another referral will come between us soon enough.

Front Facing

I play golf with a retired attorney. As he helped search for my ball in the woods, I asked for his opinion on referrals.

"I built a very lucrative practice on referrals alone. If I had a hole in my calendar, I would call a referral source in New York City to let them know I'd be in town on Thursday or Friday. Maybe we could meet for lunch."

He kicked my ball out from behind a tree.

"If that referral source was available, I would then buy a ticket for the two-hour train ride to the city and buy them lunch."

Stay in touch with your people.

CHAPTER 15

Network

Action creates referrals.

Another way a referral collector can create their own referrals is by becoming actively involved in the community, by volunteering.

Nonprofit organizations are always looking for people like you who want to get involved.

The first rule about volunteering is to stay true to your authentic self. Then stay present.

If you have taken Spanish for three years and your friend is a member of the French Club, don't join the French Club in your senior year of high school just to add an activity to your college résumé. I may or may not have committed that crime of desperation. Get involved in the Spanish Club as a freshman and then become a leader in due time.

Volunteer for an activity, club, or group that interests you. If you like finance, offer to be on the finance committee at your church or do the books for a charity fundraiser. If you have kids, volunteer to help coach a softball or soccer team. But if you work on a political campaign, don't hang signs or bumper stickers around the office. You'll alienate half your customers.

Volunteer with the expectation of receiving nothing in return.

Show up to work. Get your hands dirty. Be active. Help where they need help. Don't sit in the back of the room or stand along the wall. Don't whine about the way they do things. Let your actions show you joined to make a change, not for the sake of joining.

When you are volunteering with a charity, organization, or sports team, remember the "hurricaneologist theory." Don't chase. Let them choose you. Don't brag about what you do.

Keep your profession to yourself. Word will get out as to your career, even if you try to hide it. As people get to know you, they may ask questions about what you do or what they should do in your particular field. Answer them honestly, without selling. Don't see them as a prospect. Avoid selling. Never close. No PSC.

Eventually, an ask will come. If you play it correctly, the constructed referral will be as sticky as the customer referral. Be humble about what you do. Don't state your title. Describe how you help solve your customers' problems with a one-line description that might generate a follow-up question.

An accountant might say, "I help people who pay their fair share of taxes but want to minimize excess payments to the government."

A roofer might say, "I'm a roofer, but I only install a new roof when the person really needs it."

The financial advisor might say, "I take the stress out of investing for moms and dads," or "I make sure my customers' money will outlive them."

Don't ask for business. Don't dominate the conversation by talking about yourself or how you helped a customer go from twenty-five dollars in savings to a million bucks and a 1969 Corvette.

If somebody asks about working with you, stick to the script. Remember the basics from our earlier chapter on first impressions. Invite your potential customer to the office to interview you. If you are providing a service such as plumbing or roofing, offer to visit them at their convenience to assess the problem.

Always develop trust first. Cement your first impression, then make it to the first date before you offer solutions and pricing.

Win-Win-Win Situation

Sometimes, someone will ask you to donate to a fundraising auction or charity event.

If you provide professional services like accounting, legal, or financial services, don't donate a $100 savings coupon for your services to a silent auction. It gives a look of desperation.

Work with your referral network instead. Ask your favorite restaurant to donate gift cards. Ask your carpet cleaner to offer a coupon for two free rooms cleaned. Help other people get the word out about their services.

By doing this, you help two parties: the nonprofit and your professional network.

CHAPTER 16

Walk Away

Sometimes your network referrals will let you down. When that happens, you should change direction.

Front Facing

I had a painter friend, Frank, who provided meticulous painting at a reasonable price. His genuine personality, depth of experience, and knowledge of local trivia made him a pleasure to meet after work for a beer. In fact, that's where he picked up much of his business.

After years of friendship and great painting, we introduced him to our first referee, a long-time customer of mine with plenty of money. Within minutes of their initial meeting, she called to tell me how much she loved him, as I would expect.

A week later, the relationship soured when he offered his opinion. Her proposed maroon paint clashed with the dining room wallpaper, so he refused to paint below the chair rail.

Frank was the first to complain to me. The referee was belligerent. She didn't know what she was talking about.

A sinking feeling started in my chest.

Then my customer's name appeared on my caller ID. That feeling sunk from my chest to my stomach. Frank disgusted her. He talked down to her. He raised his voice.

I remembered a boss who regularly reminded me, "No good deed goes unpunished."

I knew both parties well and trusted each of them. After hearing both sides of the story, I realized the old saying applied. There are three sides to any story: what he said, what she said, and what actually happened.

After salvaging both relationships, we gave Frank another chance. We introduced him to a newly married couple who wanted the entire ground floor of their first house painted. The initial meeting went well. Both parties spoke highly of each other, and both thanked me for the introduction.

I breathed a sigh of relief.

Two weeks later, the husband called to say he had never heard from Frank again. No follow-up. No estimate.

The Frank referral became asymptomatic. The downside risk to my reputation cost more than the upside benefit of helping a good customer with a fresh coat of paint on their walls.

Painters are hard to find, but Frank forced me to remove him from my referral quiver without fanfare.

It's important to realize you can't be everything to everybody. Don't refer to a painter for the sake of the referral. Only refer to the painter who will make your customer happy.

I still don't refer to painters because I haven't found one I trust.

Never risk your reputation for the benefit of a referral that doesn't provide the same quality of service as you.

CHAPTER 17

Tapestry

If you view your customers as a flock, you will eventually develop the members into a mature referral network. Your referral network will become self-sustaining, feeding your business with new customers at a steady pace. I've often compared a referral business to a quilt.

Quilting

A quilt begins with cotton or raw material. The referral process starts with a potential customer. Great first impressions transform the cotton into a thread, a single customer. As the relationship strengthens, one customer leads to another. The threads work together to form a swatch of fabric. Soon, you refer customers to other customers who are also trusted professionals within your book. Eventually, you form swatches of fabric that work together.

Referring customers to "trusted" professionals in other industries creates a broader network. Over time and with consistency, the network lives and breathes, creating more swatches in different shapes and sizes. Soon, the network becomes interdependent as the fabric swatches bind into a quilt of many colors.

As the center of influence, you construct the quilt. In return, the quilt keeps you warm.

While researching this book, I had breakfast with a Realtor friend whom I've trusted with many referrals. After hearing the quilt metaphor, she thought about it for a minute, then told me that it is more complex than that. She said, "A referral business resembles a priceless tapestry, woven over time with people and relationships, bound by trust and loyalty. It creates a unique experience, improving the lives of all involved."

After a little research, I realized she was correct.

Imagine your business as a tapestry with each thread representing a relationship—a customer, a conversation, a recommendation. On their own, the threads seem small, even fragile. But when woven together with intention, they form a strong, beautiful, and expansive pattern—a thriving business built on trust.

The Warp Threads: Your Foundation

In tapestry weaving, the warp threads run vertically. They are the backbone, held under tension. In a referral-based business, these are your core traits:

- Time—check in on your customers
- Empathy—be a good listener
- Authenticity—be yourself

These warp threads never change direction. They hold the shape of the whole piece, which is your brand.

The Weft Threads: Your Network

Weft threads run perpendicular, woven in and out of the warp, giving strength to the tapestry. These represent your relationships. Each interaction, each satisfied customer, and each referral that threads through your foundational values, expands your reach.

- One happy customer refers two friends.
- A friend of a friend hears about your service at a dinner party.
- Your effort impresses a fellow volunteer at a charity event.

Each referral weaves another line of color and connection into the tapestry, slowly building a broader and more intricate picture of your business.

Patterns Emerge Over Time

The beauty of a tapestry isn't obvious at first. Like a referral network, it grows organically, sometimes invisibly, until a pattern emerges. Whether it's a reputation, a recognizable style, or a web of trust, these patterns do the following:

- Reflect your consistency
- Tell the story of your business
- Make every relationship add a new dimension to the bigger picture

Snags And Loose Threads

In any tapestry, a pulled thread can distort the image. In a referral-based business, a bad experience or broken trust can ripple through your network. Trim those threads back. Maintaining quality, reputation, and good referrals is critical for each thread to strengthen the tapestry.

Time And People

A well-made tapestry takes thousands of hours over many years to create. Weavers work with each thread individually. Similarly, establishing a referral business takes time and effort. One by one, satisfied customers will spread the good news to their friends, family, and colleagues.

Avoid the microwave mentality. It's impossible to collect loyal and satisfied customers as fast as reheating a cold cup of coffee. Building an interdependent network of customers and referrals takes even longer. Be patient.

Legacy And Continuity

A well-made tapestry lasts generations. Similarly, a referral-based business becomes self-sustaining with consistent effort and patience. Your early customers become long-term advocates. Over time, your network weaves more lines into the tapestry, growing stronger with each connection.

A referral-based business is a living tapestry—every relationship, every gesture, every delivered promise becomes a thread. They form something greater than the sum of the parts. Empathy, authenticity, and enthusiasm become the backbone of a work of art made of trust.

Front Facing

When my Realtor friend and I finished breakfast, I asked her how my business differs from other advisors. She sipped her tea, then thought for a moment. "Dorsey, you and your people have an uncanny ability to stay in touch with people."

I never thought of it that way. We just check in with our customers. In hindsight, they take care of us as much as we take care of them.

CHAPTER 18

Water The Garden

Picture the promise of spring. Winter loosens its clench of cold weather. You can feel the days growing longer, promising warmer times ahead.

You're inspired to plant a garden, then stay with it this year. You prepare the ground and plant a few rows of tomato seeds. With a little water, they soon sprout with the promise of a tasty summer harvest. You're super excited, hopeful.

But then, life gets in the way. Maybe you join a sports league. Or practices start for your daughter's travel softball team. Perhaps you meet a hurricaneologist at happy hour.

Life gets busier. You forget to water. You don't check on your babies, your heirloom tomato plants. A few weeks later, you venture out back to check on the progress. To your surprise, the little plants have succumbed to drought. You forgot to water them, neglecting the attention they need.

This is exactly how many businesses treat their existing customers. They close the sale, move on, and only come back when they *need something*, like another sale, a referral, or a review.

Relationships, like gardens, thrive when you nurture them consistently.

Watering your garden means showing up after the customer hires you. It means checking in, adding value, sending something useful, or even just saying "thank you." When your customers feel cared for, they grow into advocates: loyal, rooted, and ready to tell their friends about you.

And just like healthy plants attract bees and butterflies, healthy relationships attract referrals. You don't have to beg for them. They bloom naturally.

So don't go chasing new fields when your own soil is dry. Water your garden. It's more profitable than starting a new garden from seed. When a gardener nurtures their own plants, they produce more fruit. In the same way, when you care for your existing customers, they will help you grow your business through referrals.

Consistent Watering = Consistent Service

A garden thrives with regular watering, not when it rains, but when you show up intentionally. The same goes for your customers. When you consistently show up with value, attention, and care *after* the sale, you build deep roots of trust. Make one thousand calls per year.

Healthy Plants Attract Pollinators = Happy Customers Attract Referrals

A vibrant garden draws in bees, butterflies, and admiration. Likewise, satisfied customers naturally talk. When their experience with you is exceptional and ongoing, they become referral "pollinators" who carry your name far and wide. Give referrals.

Neglect Leads To Wilt = Ignoring Customers Dries Up Referrals

If you only water when you're desperate for flowers, your garden won't thrive. If you only reach out to customers when you need something like a referral, they feel used. Referrals come from relationships, not transactions. Meet in person with nine people per week.

Different Plants, Different Needs = Personalized Follow-Up

Some customers want check-ins. Others want resources or recognition. Tending your garden means knowing what each "plant" needs. Personalizing your follow-up fosters loyalty and generosity. Call people when you think of them. They'll welcome the thought.

The richest referrals often bloom where you've already planted care, trust, and value. Nurture what you've already grown and watch your business flourish organically.

Final Thoughts

Don't wait to transition from a sales business to a customer-focused business built on referrals. Start today.

Eliminate the dirty words from your dialect. Don't call them "prospects." Build relationships. Ditch the product sale. Solve problems. Never close a relationship. Provide a service.

Build the foundation of your referral business with time, empathy, and authenticity. Genuinely desire to use your skills to help your customers solve their problems.

Forget pestering existing customers for the phone numbers of their closest friends and family. Avoid asking for referrals after you close the sale.

Call your customers to check in with them. Tell them you were thinking of them. Ask how they're doing. Ask about their kids. Then ask if they need to hear from you more. Never discuss service or product until you are in a formal meeting.

Imagine the surprise when your customers receive a simple check-in call with no PSC or product talk. It will solidify your reputation. They will feel more connected.

Make it a point to check in with five people a day. Stay at the front of their mind. They'll *want* to tell their friends and colleagues about you.

Don't chase. Let them choose.

Acknowledgments

I thank my father, Lew Dorsey, who inspired me to join the Navy after college. I may have disliked every moment, but it molded a discipline in me that cemented a foundation for success. As he once told me, "I wouldn't want to do it again, but I'm damn glad I did it."

I thank Joe's father, Pat Ford, who started as a furniture salesman and then retired as a successful business owner with multiple stores. His simple but powerful words about taking care of the customer still resonate with me forty years later.

About The Author

Paul grew up in the second smallest state, setting the stage for a successful career in big corporate. Catholic grade school led to an all boys college-prep school, helping him earn an NROTC scholarship to a university with a championship basketball team near Philadelphia. He also has an MBA and a master's in creative writing. After a tour on board the USS *Clark* (FFG-11), his challenges began.

It didn't take long for him to fail at his first attempt as a financial advisor, so he took an entry-level position at a small trust company started by a member of the du Pont family. American Guaranty and Trust provided him with invaluable experience, serving financial advisors from his time as a securities processor all the way to the C-suite.

During that same time, he started and failed at multiple side gigs, which included carpet cleaning, chicken cheesesteaks, a flower shop, real estate rentals, and even attempting to start another trust company. All along, he continued to invest in his education by studying the teachings of Pat Williams, Brian Tracy, Napoleon Hill, and Dale Carnegie; each of these proved to be more valuable than the tickets he punched in formal education.

At the beginning of this century, Paul worked nights and weekends for a small broker-dealer, giving financial advice to family and friends. He finally quit his real job to go independent, timing it perfectly before the 2008 financial crisis, when everybody despised their financial advisor.

Since then, he built an independent practice providing comprehensive wealth management services, including retirement planning, private investments, and trusts. He worked solely on referrals and did not discriminate between regular-net-worth, high-net-worth, or ultra-high-net-worth clients. In order to work with Paul, you needed to know somebody who knows him. In 2021, he sold his company to a mega-RIA (Registered Investment Advisor).

An accomplished writer, Paul's first novel, *Forbidden Inheritance*, was inspired by family and clients alike.

Paul finds himself in the minority at home. Every day, his wife, his two daughters, a mother-in-law, and two female dogs teach him a little more about how to improve himself. As you may imagine, he often feels as though he is drowning in estrogen.

Having built his career on the advice of many who have gone before him, Paul enjoys working with and speaking to young entrepreneurs, recent grads, and financial advisors who desire to build a referral-based practice.

You can find his author page at LPaulDorsey.com.

www.ingramcontent.com/pod-product-compliance
Ingram Content Group UK Ltd.
Pitfield, Milton Keynes, MK11 3LW, UK
UKHW040010200726
13854UKWH00001B/123

9 781966 168768